Some Acne
A diary of poetry

Ryota Akase

Ukiyoto Publishing

All global publishing rights are held by

Ukiyoto Publishing

Published in 2025

Content Copyright © Ryota Akase

ISBN 9789370097414

All rights reserved.
No part of this publication may be reproduced,
transmitted, or stored in a retrieval system, in any
form by any means, electronic, mechanical,
photocopying, recording or otherwise, without the
prior permission of the publisher.

The moral rights of the authors have been asserted.
This book is sold subject to the condition that it shall
not by way of trade or otherwise, be lent, resold, hired
out or otherwise circulated, without the publisher's
prior consent, in any form of binding or cover other
than that in which it is published.

www.ukiyoto.com

Dedication

This for that lonely college kid that wrote some of the most beautiful pieces ever written. I hope that kid knows he's 'gonna be something one day.

This one's for you, kid.

Contents

4/28/15	1
4/29/15	2
6/16/15	3
8/23/15	4
8/24/15	5
9/10/15	8
9/10/15 – 2	10
9/19/15	11
9/21/15	14
10/2/15	15
10/6/15	17
10/8/15	19
10/12/15	21
10/12/15 – deux	24
10/13/15	25
10/20/15	26
10/21/15	28
10/22/15 – preternature	30
10/22/15 – en anglais malaise	31

11/12/15	35
11/22/15	36
11/23/15	39
11/30/15	41
11/30/15 – Sucks	43
11/30/15 – Abode	45
12/8/15	46
12/9/15	47
12/8/15 – train hate	51
11/24/15 – Pour paris et pour beirut	54
12/14/15	56
12/14/15 – subconsciously	58
12/14/15 – gay	60
12/15/15	62
12/16/15 – 21:53	64
12/18/15	65
12/18/15 – you and me	66
12/20/15	68
12/20/15 – in me	70
12/21/15 – gun bam	74
12/22/15	77
12/25/15	78

12/27/15 – 23:42	79
12/31/15	81
1/8/16	83
1/10/16	84
1/12/16	86
1/13/16	87
1/18/16	89
1/18/16 – sink	91
1/21/16 – don't	94
1/30/16	96
2/8/16	99
2/10/16	100
2/23/16	102
2/27/16 – premiere	105
2/29/16	108
2/29/16 – aderol	109
2/29/16 – drugs	111
3/1/16 – furst	113
3/1/16 – hey	116
3/3/16	118
3/5/16	119
3/5/16 – way day	120

4/2/16	121
4/6/16	122
4/8/16	123
4/14/16	125
4/15/16	126
4/19/16	127
4/23/16	131
5/5/16	135
5/8/16	136
About the Author	*137*

4/28/15

I feel i've been set on fire
I feel i've been set aflame
And the story goes we're insane

I feel like the clouds are higher
I feel like the waters gone dry
And the story goes we're to blame

4/29/15

I'm a writer who can't write,
I'm pathetic - the whole she-bang
A hypocrite in the midst
Disgusting poetry- as well.

I'm beaten by those folks in W
Those hanky shits who should never write
I hate those fucks
I wish i were them

The first chapter – great
Superb, but all is an unholy writ
A goddamned script that no audience can comprehend
A potential, that is – only!

6/16/15

Insecure is myself
When will i grow up?
The time i walk on two feet
My own two feet

I wonder if they know
Of my pain and sorrow
A curse bestowed to me
I hate this life

Used to the closeted abode
A place of solitary time
Where everything is slow
Somewhere i don't need to wake up from

8/23/15

I'm in a cage with no walls
Fences have been drawn not in stone but in print
I cannot escape here
I simply cannot
-that even the brigades couldn't save me
Whilst everyone else is.

The ones i love are assholes
They locked me here
For that, i am stupified
Of the ordeal they went to imprison someone,
Who knows nothing of the world and itself
For purpose of custom and morals
Said human has become dead and deader as it grew
They have become it that they prevented it to be.

8/24/15

The saddest day in my life is today,
Skies gloomy and dark, whisking the grey
It's not really sad just somber,
I hate sobriety too!

Birds chirped in rows but forgot to change their feathers thereafter,
Pupils read and everyone sat silent yet talking in the midst.

I felt sad – just because.
A violet bag to my front and a bottle of stale water to my right.

I saw how my friends laugh at their jokes,
Jokes I found funny too,
Heard mine, as well, but only some laughed.
Then again, i'm not a comic,

Some Acne

I don't live to tell the truth,
Hated the life i'm wrought into – with a price of sand.

Everything just piled up in me, and I collapsed,
The building that is mine, has become ash!
Sad that such olden design being faded,
Not even the villainous could ever redeem!

Try as i might – all's for naught,
Laughter and fun don't work anymore,
See myself as barrier and hinder
To everyone else's joy;
But then again, everyone's spade and stone
Which is more rotten to the bone.

What is the price of happiness?!
I'd have shouted to the gods,
Queries unanswered and left to rot,
Yet has traded like the air.
The saddest part:

I never knew what caused such great sadness,

Maybe I've felt too empty like a juiceless coconut shell,

Lost of jewels and black pearls, maybe.

I could only hope for the better;

And if not - just some good weather

9/10/15

If you find someone who loves you earth and sky,
And treats you to grains of rye;
Then, you are lucky and very much at that.

None could find the funniest man,
Nor can we find the most beloved,
But we hope - we pray:
Sooner or later, we find what fate has dearly entrusted.

Snoring through the shallow fields of hay;
Is our human - the most perfect high,
Shallow in thought but sometimes may not,
Whistled through the air
We lock,
Our hands place great deal on these effects
And we swallow the finest of thee.

The oaks, yew and elm sit patiently,
They breeze my enemy with warmth
But trouble me in pass,
Tis the morning starlight becomes faceless doors,
Passed and seen at an instant,
Us are heaving, us are dried;
They catch our olden ways and bring forth novelty
And grace.

This, I have seen from eyes of flesh,
But also in my bloodied and crimson heart.

Some Acne

9/10/15 – 2

No one loves me
No one does
Worthless and untalented
I've been forsaken for my ill fault

The doors slammed shut to my face
Wall crumbled bizarre
Rain became hellfire
As tokens of joy vanished

I'll never be loved
I cannot be loved
So the story goes
I belong to where there are hoes.

9/19/15

I'm in love with an actor
Who looks like the boy in the sweater
Who i think who could weather
All my problems away

He's taken up dancing
And i felt like prancing around
Him
When he's exhausted

I'm in love with boy
Who gives me happiness
No more hazy days
Of my old sick ways

I'm in love with the actor
Who looks like from porn

Some Acne

And i will have to wake up
To accept him not scorn

I'm in love with a boy
Who gives me happiness
No more hazy days
Uhuh
No more hazy days
He gives me gold
While others just sorrow
And scorn
And i mourn
That he is
He is in love
With a girl

I'm in love with a boy
Ohhhh I'm in love with a boy
I think i should wake up and
Just stick to a simpler joy

A simpler joy

I'm in love with that boy
Ohh
Please don't turn away
I'm in love with you
I'm in love with you
I'm in love
Don't turn away
Don't leave me be
I'm in love with you boy.

9/21/15

Grief swallows every pit of my soul
I can't breathe
I couldn't swallow
I die a little

10/2/15

Damage is done
I feel fear
I have lost

They have won the game
The game is life and i lost dear
I can only
Hear
The
Whisper
Of death

That i am subsumed in pain
Yet
I feel nothing at all

That the worst is the anesthesia

Some Acne

The feeling of loss
And sorrow
In which you feel none but pain
And you feel,
Day by day,
A little more insane.

That is the worst pain.

10/6/15

Round and round i go
The turntables were a house
The carousel was alive

I peered up at the sky and it was different from what i thought it was
I saw a grandfather cradling a small child

Then i took a peer again and it was gone
Replaced by somethin' else

I walked the dog
Straight we went and he waggled his tail
As i thought and pondered my tale

The sun was lisping
The shadows were appearing

Some Acne

The path was darkening and shady and hollow

We went back where we came
I saw the same clouds
But they're dead now
What a shame

A looked at the dog
And he went aloof
High on the meadowy dandelion patches
I teared in the form of air

10/8/15

I have come to realize faith
It took heart and soul
Yet it still miles away

Lookin' greatly in forth
I can crawl

Able to walk two by two
Feet left and right
I do

They smiled at me as i did
I did what i was
And it was alright

Finally a sense i've lost
Raw in vapor

Some Acne

And it wasn't dust

I am confused my dear foe
In love and yet in hatred
I really am

What joy will it deduce on me
As i crawl towards my epiphany

That i see lights in the midnight sky
Neither the stars nor the moons

Which of which
I am happy to know
Happy really happy
That sludge has melted into snow

10/12/15

Circles taper her gentle
Her lips sealed and pasted
Of honey and lies
All of our sweet good byes

Far from cityscapes and hours
Hours, hours away
That she smiles sweetly
But thinks devilishly

She walked by the door
And then stopped

She paused to wither
And yet stop short of fade

They inside chatting

Some Acne

Laughing at the blue
The blue buying the night
For her an accursed night

Tear after tear it fell
Each one a story to tell
That fine art is crooked
And wisdom frequently bended

Time has come for her
For her time extended arm
Her kohl dried in a line
And a wet sight to divine

Come my dear come
And she did
The night did shiver
And her lips didn't

It was a sight to unbeholden

Of lovers and broken

Th—

10/12/15 – deux

Don't you know how perfect we'd be
For each other
That the stars above could not compare
Not even our greatness can be blown by air

I want you to feel it too
These feelings that i have for you
That when the dogs howl
Whence felines make love
That i am in love
With you

Hoping every day for your attention
That you give me time with intention
Grab my consciousness with earnest
To make me fall because you have
As well.

10/13/15

At first i disliked you
Then i started to tolerate you
And then i started to like you
In the end i fell in love with you

One way or another
My love for you grew much brighter
Not even the sun can compare

One thing is we got separated
Then we got alienated
You started to head your way
While in the thought of you blissed out of my day

One thing's for sure
You never lost the allure
That makes me feel so demure
And like my feelings are the same as manure

10/20/15

All my dreams are gone
I can't be an actor
A poet
A lover
A child
Nor even human

I'm confined by the walls for those like me
And all of them have either died
Or comatosed

In this forsaken world

That i cannot acquire beauty in the bounty of technology
That i cannot act for the simpleness of drama

What can i do?
I have lost hard
My soul is tardied
And the music dead

How can i strive
For a better life?
When life itself strives
Struggles
For a better me.

10/21/15

I wish spanish is spoken again
As the first of over half the people

I know it sounds absurd
You have a great language
Gender neutral and flexible
Very recommendable
But still

I do wish to hear Neruda by the shore
Or Octavio by my neighbor's snore

That i walk within surrealist realm
Of absurdity and banal
Things falling into

Walking among vine clad walls

With dancing steel verandas
Of eccentricity
In art
In poetry which is bizarre

That songs be emotional and passionate
That i float in the hurdle of the feeling
See stars in the bright daylight
Even if i know that dreams fall.

10/22/15 – preternature

With the fusion of heat
I due in time
Wings behold
Shattered and taped together
What goes for its triumph?

10/22/15 – en anglais malaise

What ails me is me
What isn't mine is mine

That like problems are like mine when
Whence they aren't

Sad but true
I question the gods of such building
Development that isn't good
Such have been discouraged

But look at the word
Discourage
Dis-courage
To fall out of bravery and
And sell ourself

Some Acne

That's what i feel -discouraged
The help books could not help
Not even the beauty of the outside could
As well

What will i do?
Towards change in self
To make more attractive
Thy exterior without nudity
Nor exposure
What?
Maybe
I think it is
Death
Stoppage of my heart beats
The source of this sorrow
My heart
Must be stopped
But i am
Powerless

Powerless to do something
And i die
Without ever having felt it

I have died
Because i was simply discouraged

It wasn't the economy
The society i live in
The family nor community
It was me
I was responsible
And i became the opposite.

Some Acne

Somewhere in 2015 – fuck – me – ?

Fuck me Good

Fuck me good
Fuck me tender
This fuckery ails me
Baby

11/12/15

You can't see the stars when it fall like rain

11/22/15

I have a hard time believing you
I hate when I feel like this

Fuck, what I feel for you
You're lucky I can even allow this

I see you enjoying your life
But what do you think of me

I bet you don't and I hate that
I hate that specific factoid buzzin in my head

Sometimes I can write for hours
On end, I can think of verses just due to you

When will this suffering end
I wish it was soon or just now - please

I'm usually strong and might
My eyes wouldn't even bat for a second

I could say you are the opposite of me
You see things bright and straightforward

I don't

I cry sometimes and I wail for my mother
I hope you don't but a part of me wishes though
I sleep a lot and hate to move
You dance and groove

The paper and note is my leisure
While yours is friends and dance

You're pretty content in your life
And that's where we differ
Where you see the rainbow and the sun and the sky

Some Acne

I see blood and the darkness of the night

When you feel like you could shoot to the sky
I just desire to get the slumber of time afar

I guess we weren't made to be, huh
That all things add to your difference
The difference which is to me
Unbreakable and simply, hopeless

11/23/15

Subconsciously, I am sore
Head to toe – in constant pain
Sighing in this morning as I rise
I dread, yes, I dread

The morning's cool and pale
Something must have been
I don't know
The memories keeps whistling back
Howling tremendously
The last hour even, I had a dream

On my way to the cinema
Futurism abounded the foyer
The neon lights and the steel interiors
It spoke coolly to me
Saying that the hours have left me by

Telling that the world would simply pass by
I could not bear this though
So I think that is why I want to walk in the snow

11/30/15

Would you leave him?
Would you be with me instead?
Would you leave her?
What about me?

I love you in reality
In love like paste to your shard
Is it that i am hopeless?

I'm disgusting
I know
From everyday I'm taught that

Shut up shut up
Please just quiet
I don't wanna know no more
You just hate me

Fuck my life
Fuck it all
You can't answer me
Like you can't even stand me

11/30/15 – Sucks

All my power is from you
God you're so beautiful
Your hair your smile
The way you talk
Your walk and the way you are

The class would mind
That if i am in yours
Sadly they would
Not to mention
You might as well

Sucks that you aren't mine
And i'm not yours
Freedom is despicable
If slavery is equal to you

That i wake in your bed
With you and your pretty head
Snoozing the day away
As i just watch and lay
The beautiful man i fell for
Poems and all connected us
But something we lacked we did

And here i end
Staring at the phone
And i can hone the passiveness of thee
For ignorance of you never loving me

11/30/15 – Abode

We often get lost in our debauchery
Forgetting the sequencing of paying for this abode

12/8/15

Take the subway
And go, now
See the stars
That shine below

12/9/15

Hello my love
The love i yearn
At your constern

Let us eat
In splendor of life
Which you give me
By making me love thee

The sadness ripped
Up in the shreds
And joyful once more

Yuletide ne'er bring much
But thou presence sure

When you greet me

Some Acne

I smile
Like a child seeing new presents
And like ne'er before

Unresolved is some
My problems alone
You love me no
You do not

Please just love me
I beg you
I tear in knees
Please

In tears
I cry in sorrow
Slumber is the joy
And the living in me
Long dead so
I walk away

You do not chase
Nor do you call
You simply look
On and on

The accordions play
Romance in the fog
Dreary as a frog
Imaginary life
Like one midnight
In the city of lights

The snows trudges my boot
Both are wet
Frozen too
I tear little now
Merry kindred songs
While i am whisked away
Palms now sweating
Freezing by waist

Some Acne

Chained around
Like a serpent

Why does it begin
Ne'er the query
Always the end
But not the start

I enter the hole
That built for mine
The light turned on
And the place spotless
I silently sob
Whence i'm alone
Without them
Beside me
Where i want them
To be

12/8/15 – train hate

I hate the train
Never on time
Even for a day
They promise
They leave soon
But leave for us
They do not
Why does it
Do like that
Where we hurt
The pain courses
We are left
And loved afar
Then we forget
We ever had nothing
But now we move
Onward and on

Some Acne

I still miss it
The befores of life
Before things had
Suddenly changed
Had fell apart
Been forgotten
Become estranged
I talk to them

Still do so
Every so often
But by letters
Only words
No face nor voice
Just arts and letters
Not even a heart
Beating is heard
Life could have
It could yet
It has not though

I do not know
What it might
To feel cradling
To live again
To cry by some
To feel loved so
With them near
And i still clear
Of drama or shit

Please turn it **back**
Please turn the **time**
Turn it back
Please turn it back

11/24/15 – Pour paris et pour beirut

Hey

We love you over there

We do

We care about you

We really do

Sometimes we don't show it much

But we do

You might feel alone and sad

Remember

Youve got a friend from halfway the world

A friend from caring islands

Don't lose hope

And if you
We are always here to cheer you

12/14/15

I search for you
Left and right
The back and front
Hidden and seen
Where are you
My love?

I saw your troop
You weren't there
I saw the place
But you were out of it
Where have you gone
You should be here by now

I knew the time
The place to be
The class you are in

The people you are with
But I guess I don't know
Everything about you
Not even you

That even with the knowledge I have
The smarts and the timing
You're still not here
Not still with me

12/14/15 – subconsciously

Saw you
You were talking funny
You talked and talked
With someone else

Fuck you
You went another way
Turn around!
Why?
Why?
I love you

Lost you
The opposite you went
I am saddened
Why don't you talk to me
That way?

The way you talk to friends
The most valued of yours
Which I am not part of
Though I wish to be
Unsuccessfully

12/14/15 – gay

He's gay
The one you talked to
I think so

You hang out with other gay people
Yet why not me?
Why hang with that stupid hoe?
Who thinks he's all that
Like he is
He looks like shite
Not even a pretty sight
He thinks he's all that
That he's beautiful and cute
But never either just neither

He's had other people
But for me

You'll be the only
He found three in succession
I never did though
Never have I

I can't have you
That's clear
Carols rang the plaza
While I waste in your parade
I wish I had you
Even if there's difficult water to wade

12/15/15

I'd have never met you
If I was born elsewhere
Like france
Where i could've found another

It sucks that you
Don't love me
Maybe in sweden or germany
You would

What else do i have
Canada, finland, netherlands
All could've given me a life
A love life

Maybe in geordie
Or in argentina

Maybe even in uruguay
Could have even answered
The most troubling of why's

I don't know what to do
New zealand
Maybe the place
To not know you
Even colombia or brazil feels better
Or even norway or denmark too

I think of Iceland
The place is far
Far from you
Why not go there
And move on from you

12/16/15 – 21:53

I like that it lightly drizzles at night

I see snippets of dark and snippets of bright

Even though all I could see were lamp posts shining contrite

12/18/15

Cracked skin pulped with hair
Absinthe
Pinkwashed walls and white tiles
Precinct

12/18/15 – you and me

You'd get tired of me
I know that

You'd never love me
I knew that

You'd forget me
I expect that

You'd ignore me
I expected that

You'd hate me
I predict that

You'd resent me
I predicted that

You'd leave me
I know so

You'll never love me
So much so

12/20/15

I wish i could delete emotions

Love

Sadness

Care

All that hurts

They're useless anyway

They make you

Fear

Regret

Remorse

Shameful

All that makes tears

Painful memories is what they always bring to me

Like those of

My childhood

My teenage years
My crushes
My achievements
All they do is make me look back

And i am pained by that
That i have to
Watch
See
Feel
Hear
Anticipate
Losing the people i love

All because i was weak
All because i had these emotions
All because
All because

12/20/15 – in me

You told me we were gonna be together
You told me
You told me

No you didn't
You didn't
You promised me though
In my dreams
In my dreams

You were clear there
I cried while i wrote this
Because it felt
It felt real
It was real
At least to me
It was
12/21/15 – pretty boy

Where have you gone my pretty boy?
I lay here restless, awake
Why would you do this?
Leave me hanging
Without a yellow and a gray goodbye

Our last conversation was ages
It was shit too
Do you remember it?
Do you recall?
I do clearly, i really do

What have you done though?
I am alone now
Maybe just like you wanted me
Yearning for a fantasy embrace
Given by you when it's cold and it rains

Hey! Is this your game?

Some Acne

Are you punking me?
Playing with me by
Ignorance, subtlety and fuck –
Everything!

Why can't you just say it to my face?
You don't love me!
You don't like me!
Heck, you don't care for me like that!
No, you just grab my attention and leave me wanting more
While you go out of it and focus on another

God, I hate you!
And fuck, I love you too!
I am officially stupid!
I could scream but who'll hear me?
You? People in the neighborhood?
They don't care
Maybe you don't too

Well, you got out of second year good
While I just wait around for subtle signs again
From ignoramus you
And lay I may in my misery
Maybe that's what you're also to me?

12/21/15 – gun bam

Holding a gun
I thought to myself
Just a couple inches or so

It was long
And hard
Sleek, metallic
Pointed in my mouth
Inches fro

I fantasized of my end
What will it be?
A bullet to the head?

I'm too old for this shit
Too old, too old
Even seniority is required

I am ugly
And fake
I know as much
Pondered as well
Though I am far fro

How could I be happy?
Even it needs fulfill
To make the cut

Forgetting is so short
Juxtaposed from myself
And also, themselves

I cannot
Also can never
Understand
The workings of my mind
Why feel this?

Some Acne

When it feels like shit?
Like the bathroom after others
Move in
And then, I pull the trigger
And bam.

12/22/15

I am so disappointed
So much so
I am so frustrated
Too much too

Why this happen?
Am I not good enough?
I think you have someone better
Goodbye then, ciao.

12/25/15

Fake smiles
Fake life

Fake face
Fake joy

Fake ignorance
Fake spacing

Fake love
Fake interest

Fake talk
Fake jokes

Fake things
Fake attempts

12/27/15 – 23:42

Whenever life is dark and blight
And when the *lampposts die* (or *flames go die*)
There is still hope
There is still life
From the old passed times
(*passed* pronounced as *pas*-**SED**)

Whichever path this life may choose
Whichever
Left or right
Even the darkness fade to light
And the day comes in bright

For hope and love
My friends
My fellow living souls
For hope and love

For peace and joy
For all and everyone

We hold on thee
We hold on tight
We hold our hearts
Up high (or *We hold*)
We hold this to be real and right
And hold our world *<u>to light</u>* (or *on bright*)

For peace always came with good
And the soul in our lives
Let's hold each other
Real tight
And brace the **darkness' blight** (or **darkening night** [*darkening* pronounced as *dark'ning*])

12/31/15

Hey, it's the new year
A year without snow
A year in love with you

It's good nowadays
I feel better
Yet I see myself sadder
And you and I farther

How have you been though?
Had a nice brunch with family?
Dinner at the strike of midnight?

I hope you did
You love your family
I can see in media
You do

Some Acne

From pictures and posts
To maybe the things you do most
You're happy
For that, I'm happy for you

1/8/16

Hey you

I'm sorry

I feel like i've been unfaithful to you

Even though i don't have you

I still care about you

1/10/16

I wrapped round your neck

We lock

Lips on lips

Both four eyes closed

I sigh

Amused

Confused

Why think of such?

At first i thought of trains

Underground

Elevated

Monorail

Nerdy train obsessed stuff

Then schmucked into thinking

Of you

Why torture myself?
Aren't i tortured enough
I dreamed we had a chance
A light in your eyes
As you figured
And you wanted too
But awake
You didn't

Why would you do back?
Love me back and just do
I can't grip you
I can't make you love
Love like me making poems
Or artists doin' art
I can't spontaneously
It's hopeless
So why bother?
Why do?

1/12/16

Amounting to a day
That's what we were

Amounting to a day
That's what I am to you

Amounting to a day
That's the times we spent

Amounting to a day
That's how I'm just worth to you

1/13/16

I'm such an ugly stupid bitch
I wish i was just a witch
So i could cast a spell on you
To make you love me too

But i can't
I love you so much
That caging you with me
Would be as killing a young dog
Unforgivable and cruel

I'll be happier to look from afar
As i reminisce the days, mornings
Of our conversations - big or small

And tears wade down my face
And as you laugh with your lover

I'll always feel that for you to be replace?
There will be no other

1/18/16

Money money
It is funny
That you torture me

You took my mother
My brothers
And my life

You barred me from my life
My friends
And the things i love

You are an A plus asshole
That I shit
When you are near

You know that i can die

Some Acne

Without you
You old two-way sword

You must really die
Or else just be redundant
I just want you gone

You'll be back with fury
Punishing me
When you wrong me

You should just leave
I hate you so
That you are my only foe

1/18/16 – sink

I just wanna cry
I'm so lonely
You'll never want me
I just let it sink

Why won't you love me?
Am i so ugly
I know i am
Maybe that's it

But uglies get love alot
They marry and have kids
Travel the world
And kiss in Paris

Maybe i'm dumb
You don't like dumb people

Some Acne

Maybe you don't
But i might be wrong

Dumbasses get love
The rich kind
And the best ones
But i don't know

I feel it's because i'm shy
You like the attention
Obviously you do
But i scorn it

Some don't love it too
And they get love
A real whole lot too
Why can't i?

Is because i'm tall?
Am i too tall for you?

I feel i am
Like a giant bear

Maybe you don't like me
Ever at all
That it's only those
Pretty girls
That make you fall

Well sometimes i feel shit
Because i don't have a vag
For you to like
And also a rack to caress

Maybe you just think of me
As a friend
Friendzone i know
Whenever i think about it
My heads hung low

1/21/16 – don't

Don't fall in love
It's a trap

Don't let someone in when they aren't the same
It's a trap

Don't give so much and expect little back
It's a trap

Don't hope so much on fantasy
It's a trap

Don't believe in love
It's a trap

Don't ever look at small things as big signs
It's a trap

Don't try showing your feelings
It's a trap

Don't ever open up to that person
It's a trap

Don't waste your time on them
It's a trap

Don't get used to being their friend
It's a trap

Don't ever fall in love
Its' a trap

1/30/16

Little boy blue
At night i watch you coo
Sometimes when your other dad's around
He watches you too

We love the random smiles in your sleep
The light snores you give
If i had all the might on the planet
I'd take every ember to keep

Sometimes you wake us
And were lazy to get
You sometimes annoy us with your crying
But we won't change any
Even when we're dying

Other times you wake us up

You demand breakfast and an apple in a cup

When you mess around we clean you
We bathe and wash the mess out of you
Even when were messy too

Sometimes i'm sad for no reason
Then you bound to me
And you give me a good reason

Others i hug you close
We sleep in the floor
Or the bed or the couch
And wait for dad for when he comes home

We kiss your cheek
Sometimes at the same time
Because you laugh and giggle
Sometimes you babble and slime
I can't wait to love you

Some Acne

Little boy blue
My little boy blue
Our very own little boy blue

2/8/16

I just wanna hide away
Tucked in my own room
Under the blankets
Far from all these eyes

They expect me at their tables
Serving them dearly
Like a false freeperson
Or a cattle for slaughter

I wanna get out
I can't live for other but never for myself
It's unfair
It is unfair
That i have to live
Just so others can too
So what if i wasn't
Am i a criminal and a fou?

2/10/16

Hey beautiful boy
Please notice me
Look at me and smile at me
Talk to me with sense

I love when you talk
It feels like angels and horns
Like love without all the thorns

I can see you
You know
Though maybe you can't see me
I'll let you free

We crossed paths again
Met by the rooms in the hall
Though this time its wasted

Cause we just greeted instead

No more how was i
Not even a small meaningful hi
Maybe this story's meant for goodbye
I'll just let this die

2/23/16

I dreamt of you
It was a foolish dream
I had it vague
I had it sour
It was a prediction
Of the coming hour

You weren't mine there
I wasn't yours
I was still alone
Faced with a rack of crap
And shit to face

But i felt that you left me
In my dream
I was foolish
And naïve to love

Someone higher than me

It was truly just stupidity
That i fell for you
A poor pauper
Looking like a fool
While i stared at the prince
With a hasty drool

I desire you
My prince charming
Your kindness, smile
Your whole
I wanna be with you

Even though
You may have your flaws
Maybe might've broken
Some of our laws
I still am

Some Acne

Hopelessly in love
With only you

2/27/16 – premiere

I wait for you
Here in where i saw you
You were facing against me
I thought still beautiful

Your hair
Looks soft
And tender and thrilled
A dancer like you should

The jacket and the cap
They fit you
I can almost imagine you
Being a dad to ours

Oh god, i'm so lovestruck
With the thought of you

That wispy daydreams
Involving you being true

I curse that the world cannot
But i thank the heavens for everything
That life gives somber
The notice
That little dreams of you
My fantasy lover

2/27/16 – where
You never came
Where were you?
I think you didn't wanna see me there

I know you like her
You wish her skin
Never mine

You brought her in school

Showed her around
Talked about and shit

Just tell me
Face to face that
You don't love me

You couldn't care less
If i died
In front of you

You shouldn't be
I'm not worth nothing
I'm never worth it

That being said
I may request one thing
One pretend kiss
To end my dreaming

2/29/16

Did friends stop into hello
Did we forget beyond, below
I can't believe you have it in
That you see me dim

Where do we start anew
Where do birds get the flu
Maybe that's where we know were through

When did farewell became unwell
When do lovers ring their bell
Twas good with you
But i just wasn't meant for you

2/29/16 – aderol

I grabbed a leaf of agno
Maybe because i love you so

I blew hot breath to the skies
Maybe because i care for so

I sought a job at a convenience store
Maybe because i miss you so

I found the treasure beneath the sea
Maybe because i want you to know me

I just walked a senior across the street
Maybe because i want you to see me

I fed my niece chocolate sundaes
Maybe because you sadden me

Some Acne

I bought my nephew a lego toy
Maybe because you ruin me

I aced the tests on psychology
Maybe because i think i'm crazy

I just wanna forget you
Maybe because you slowly kill me

2/29/16 – drugs

I need aderol
For the pain you cause
In which heroin's insufficient
In relieving the scarring

When we get weed
Ill escape to my dreams
Away with crack from you
Thats what i need to do

I can't stomach the vodka
For your love tastes bitter
Not even the opium
Away from your doom

Love me like coke
Overdosed and fraughted

Some Acne

When i ecstasy on you
I see no other

Like the crystal on my arms
Injected in haste and need
To escape your adhesive
That grabs me dear

I wanna escape
Without all these drugs
But i can't find a way
Just to get away
3/1/16
I am so much stronger now frankly yes i am
I don't want to be lonely tonight

3/1/16 – furst

I imagined getting my first with you
You pushed me into a stall
Kissed me passionately
With saliva and tongue and all

I held in my palms
Your flawless face
You were just fucking perfection
You give me the best

Tasting so good
I opened my mouth and let you roam
Touching the right places in my body
You treated me like i dreamed of

I let go for air and tire
You looked into my eyes smiling

Shyness in your façade
I delved back into our war

You leaned your head slightly
I did as well
Feeling your arms on my back
You held closer even tighter

I felt like you wouldn't let go
Like you wouldn't be one of those men in my life
All of them left or shitted on me
I wish i haven't said sooner

Soon it turned ugly
You never loved me
You just wanted to waste your time with someone
Oh i was just stupid

It wasn't how i thought it to end
I thought it would be confessions

Not aberations nor relocations
I imagined that you left me and i cried

You were the one
I gave you a piece of me i never gave others
A piece i held dear for so long
Thought i found that person
Then it was farewell already.

3/1/16 – hey

Hey you dancer boy
I miss you

Hey you dreamer boy
I miss you

Hey you kisser boy
I miss you

Hey you handsome boy
I miss you

Hey you beautiful boy
I miss you

Hey you school boy
I miss you

Hey you heartthrob boy
I miss you

Hey you big boy
I miss you

Hey you popular boy
I miss you

Even if this one don't mean nothing

Hey you lover boy
I'm in love with you
Even if you don't too

3/3/16

Stupid child
Never knowing what is what
Acts like a twat
Ends up in a knot

3/5/16

In the sun merry

And everything's forgotten and i know you hate that
(me and you always and forever)

Drops of jupiter

I started a joke and started the world crying

God only knows what i've been without you

3/5/16 – way day

Finally i've decided
That it's the end of the day
Time to stop going
Towards your way

4/2/16

Thought you were different
Thought you were good
I thought only the best of you
Then i was stabbed in the hood

4/6/16

Hello brutalist masonry
I endure your profound ugly
Your lack of care from such
That droplets of rain turn to dust

4/8/16

Let the children lose it
Would you use it

Rebel rebel
David
Bow's in your E

Acceptable bastard
You'd know
That children
Need some bait

You bastard
Harassment ain't cool
Somebody does

Portions of heaven

Some Acne

Cut for love
Windows don't matter to me

I just wanna be free
Who i look like?

Blue sky dies
And does I –

4/14/16

It's fine
Maybe it's the end
I hope you're happy
You might not be
But for what it's worth
I was happy
Now it's over
And done

4/15/16

Done being lied to
Done being neglected
Done being used for
Done being a friend

Done even caring
Done even to hope
Done knowing nothing
Done and done to no

4/19/16

I lost a dream
I lost my grand old magic dream
A city where sprite flows down the stream
It's sad to say
I lost my dream

I had this dream
Big bullions given to the poor who cannot dream
That roses grew on the windows and in the sills
I lost a dream

I lost my dream
Where we showed the people what it doesn't seem
That people walk
That they pass by and they beam
I lost my dream

Some Acne

I lost my dream
I lost a dream
It's so sad to see the ending near
That end is where it all just dims
And the curtains fade the clouds

I lost a dream
I lost a dream about how you cannot seem
To grasp the bluish angel here
Dirty, i lost a dream

I lost my dream

Look my bloody window shield
That mirror shows another fiend
I just, i lost my dream

I lost a dream
I lost a dream
My song fades into my bloody screen

Popping red and disgusting
I close my eyes
I lost a dream

When will it end
When will it be heard and read
When is it gonna face the bed
When is it gonna sound like it seemed

I lost a dream
I lost a magical fantasy
My dream of becoming a hearty fiend
Where is my dream

I lost a dream
I lost, i lost, i lost a dream
Where flowers flew in the breeze
I lost
I lost my dream
I lost

I lost it
Don't make me trouble
Because i've already lost my dream

4/23/16

Little girl fly away
Spread your wings
Even on a rainy day
Cause the city always weeps

Little girl walkin home
I know you're in this god foresaken crucible
That you only ever seem to think

What good does it bring
Thinking endlessly
I know it could be a ball
If you just remembered history

Little girl trying to climb
On the neighbor's front porch

Forgot that there's always a door

Little girl ridin the tram
I know what it feels to be rammed
Your life is in the seam baby

What does it ever hold
To love somebody
You can never fold
That finished laundry dies with me

On the pantry
Silly girl
Climb up and save the world
Can you ever do that for me?

Little girl don't be shy
I know that life ain't always right
That songs don't burst out from the trees

Little girl don't you die
That silly rockin chair don't ever sigh
They only
Only wait for thee

What does it ever go
That two stars means you're in a row
That lurking gators
Don't want to feed

What does it ever know
That silly people just love the troll
But never ever rock the dream

(Interlude)

So

Little girl don't be scared
I could show you all the stars

That ever bared
Little girl it's alright
Cause you're with me

5/5/16

I see you
I fucking see you
Everywhere

I hear you
I fucking hear you
Anywhere

I remember you
I fucking remember you
All the time

I feel you
I fucking feel you
Nowhere

5/8/16

You still here
I'm still queer

You left back
I'm still whack

You still dead
I'm still dread

You still hot
I'm still not

You still awesome
I'm still lonesome

About the Author

Ryota Akase

Ryota Akase is a Filipino siraulo (crazy head) who writes poetry on their spare time. They live in the suburbs of Manila and likes to have their alone time in the hussle and bustle of Cubao. When they're at home, the family dog is a playmate but doomscrolling is becoming a bigger contender as a pastime. They don't know what they want to do in life so they want to do everything (stupid head). Currently in between jobs, they like to draw and photograph the most striking graphics in the street and on the internet. They also made their cabinet doors their biggest sketchbook ever. They like learning languages and can understand French but can never respond in it. All in all, they are the definition of someone who just wants to live life and not be bothered with it – a true Gen Z auteur.

www.ingramcontent.com/pod-product-compliance
Lightning Source LLC
LaVergne TN
LVHW041607070526
838199LV00052B/3020